s i h v l

a W e

o j n y x

b z r

f i

V T d

q c y u

W k t g P m

All Around the Block

For Pascal — for 'inspiration';
with love to you and your
loving parents.

My very best wishes to
you three.
x Judy Pelikan

All Around the Block

an alphabet by Judy Pelikan

David R. Godine · *Publisher*
Boston

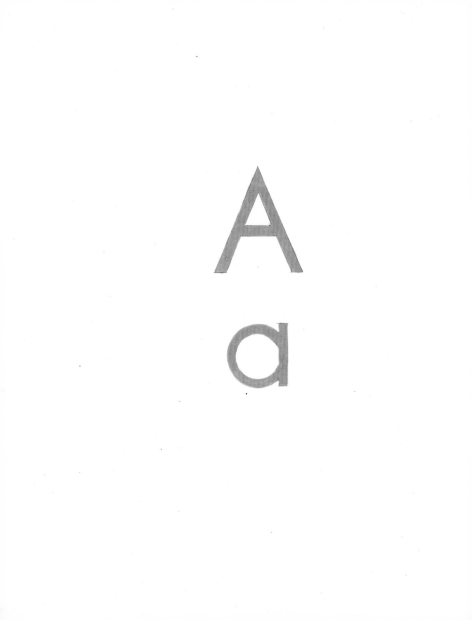

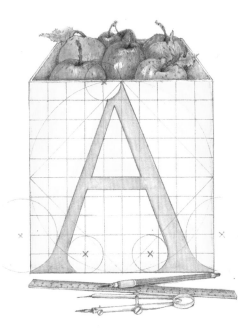

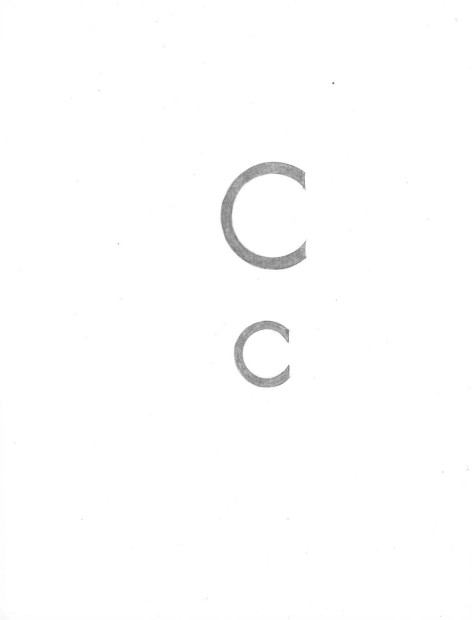

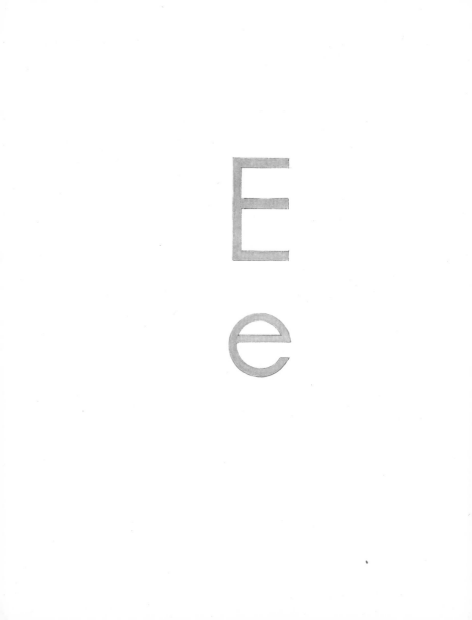

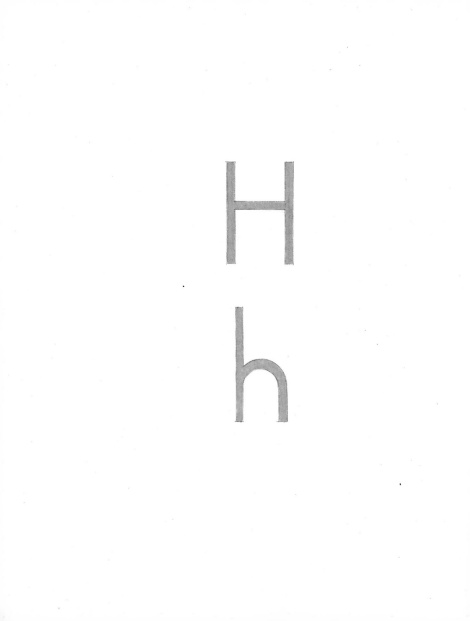

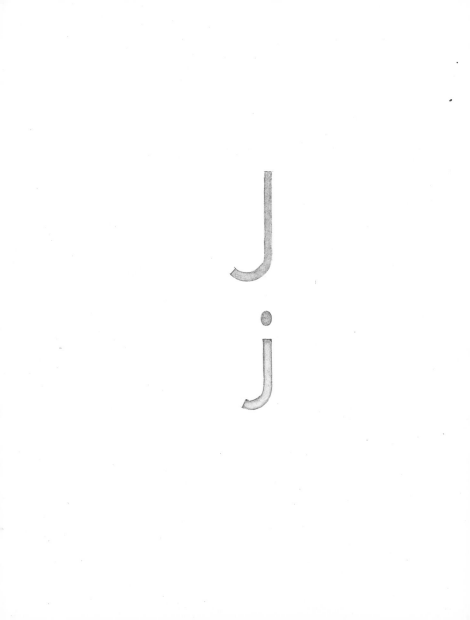

K

k

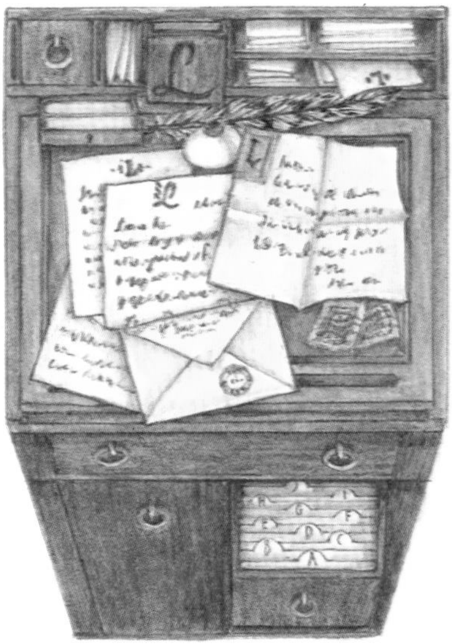

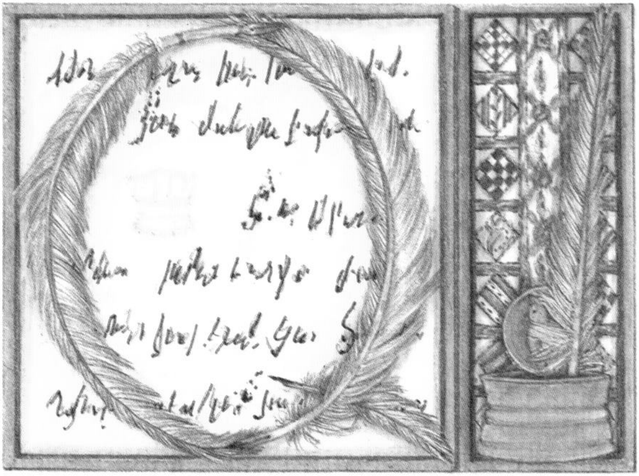

UNION JACK

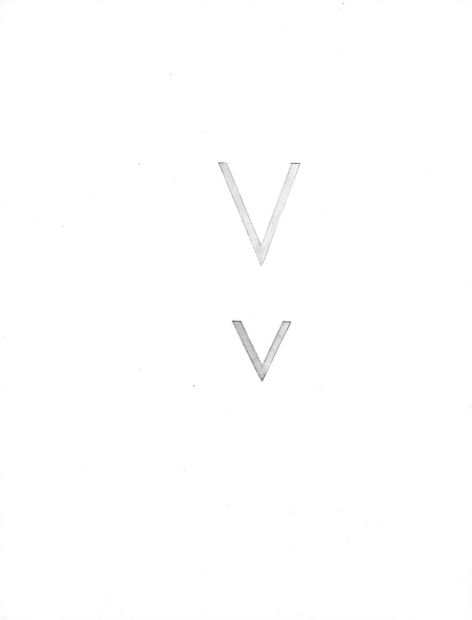

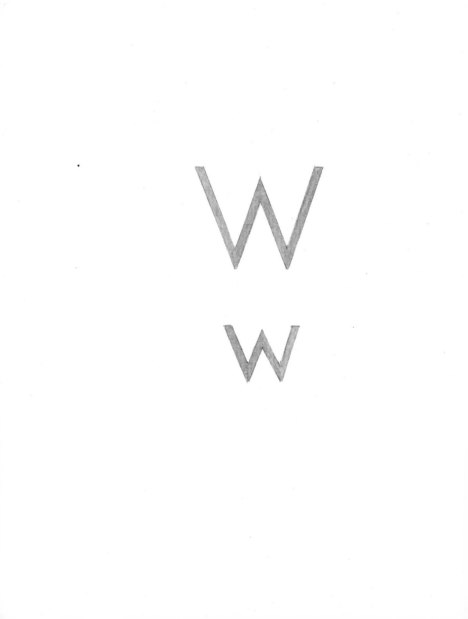

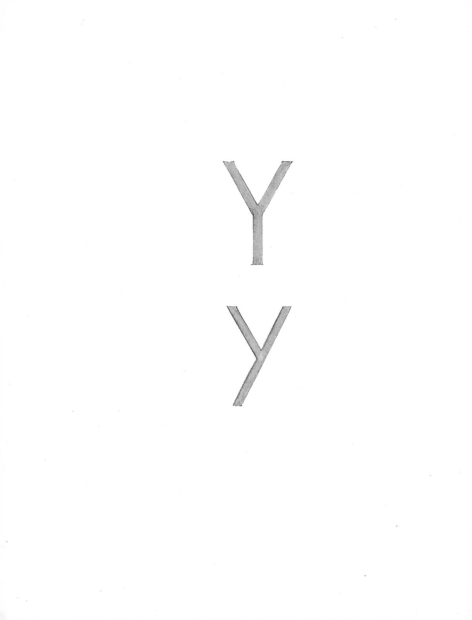

First published in 2008 by
David R. Godine · *Publisher*
Post Office Box 450
Jaffrey, New Hampshire 03452
www.godine.com

First Edition
Printed in China